Smythe Gambrell Library

Presented by

Virginia Catherine Cushing
(Class of 2013)
and
Robert Cushing
(Class of 2016)

Pollution

by Helen Orme

Consultant: Terry Johnson, Ph.D.
Educational Consultant

BEARPORT
PUBLISHING

New York, New York

Credits

Cover and Title Page, © Ben Osborne/Stone/Getty Images; Credit Page, © JustASC/Shutterstock; 4–5, © Adisa/Shutterstock; 5, © nialat/Shutterstock; 6–7, © Sai Yeung Chan/Shutterstock; 7, © egd/Shutterstock; 8, © Ian MacLellan/Shutterstock; 9, © Martin Harvey/Gallo Images/Getty Images; 10–11, © AP Images/David Guttenfelde; 12, © AP Images; 12–13, © Chris Wilkins/AFP/Getty Images; 14–15, © vera bogaerts/Shutterstock; 15, © Wendy Slocum/Shutterstock; 16–17, © Martin Green/Shutterstock; 17, © Phil Degginger/Alamy; 19, © Vlade Shestakov/Shutterstock; 20, © Hywit Dimyadi/Shutterstock; 20–21, © Mike Abrahams/Alamy; 22, © JustASC/Shutterstock; 22–23, © maigi/Shutterstock; 24T, © Michael Svoboda/Shutterstock; 24B, © Roca/Shutterstock; 25, © Christine Gonsalves/Shutterstock; 26, © melkerw/Shutterstock; 27, © Robert J. Daveant/Shutterstock; 28, © John Cancalosi/Rex Features; 29, Courtesy of the Commonwealth of Australia; 30, © Kenneth V. Pilon/Shutterstock.

Every effort has been made to trace the copyright holders, and we apologize in advance for any unintentional omissions. We would be pleased to insert the appropriate acknowledgments in any subsequent edition of this publication.

The Earth in Danger series is printed on recycled paper.

Library of Congress Cataloging-in-Publication Data

Orme, Helen.
  Pollution / by Helen Orme.
    p. cm. — (Earth in danger)
  Includes index.
  ISBN-13: 978-1-59716-724-6 (library binding)
  ISBN-10: 1-59716-724-X (library binding)
  1. Pollution— Juvenile literature. I. Title.
TD175.O76 2009
363.73— dc22
                    2008023660

10|11 363.73 Orm
SGL48060
$ 18.95

Contents

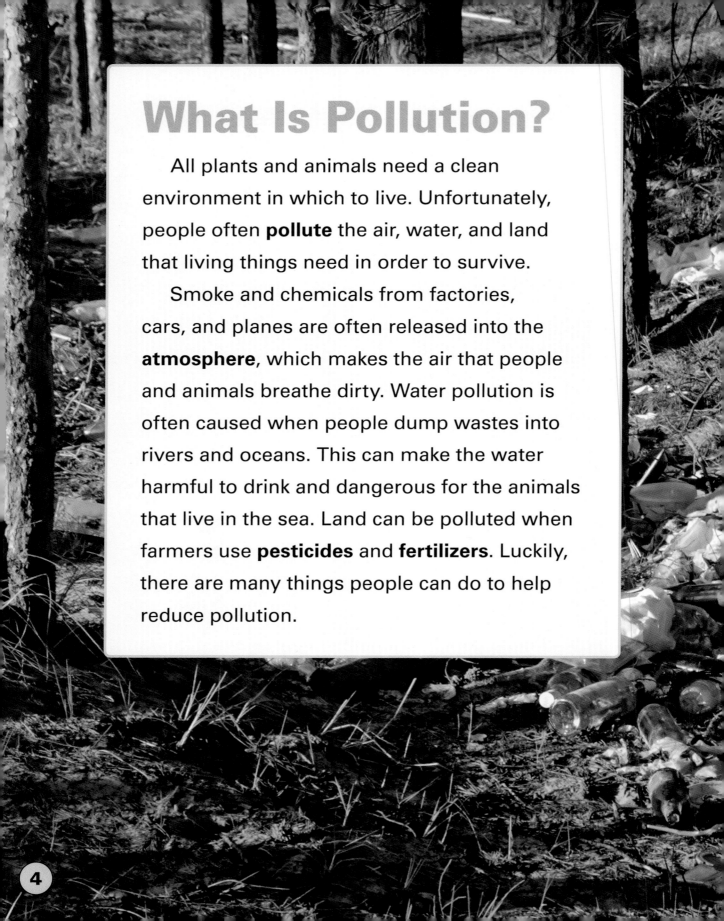

What Is Pollution?

All plants and animals need a clean environment in which to live. Unfortunately, people often **pollute** the air, water, and land that living things need in order to survive.

Smoke and chemicals from factories, cars, and planes are often released into the **atmosphere**, which makes the air that people and animals breathe dirty. Water pollution is often caused when people dump wastes into rivers and oceans. This can make the water harmful to drink and dangerous for the animals that live in the sea. Land can be polluted when farmers use **pesticides** and **fertilizers**. Luckily, there are many things people can do to help reduce pollution.

Pollution can be very deadly to animals. By 1940, for example, the number of bald eagles in the United States dropped to very low levels. A scientist discovered the cause—the birds were eating animals poisoned by a chemical that farmers were spraying on their crops. The chemical caused the eagles' eggs to be so thin that the babies inside often died before they even hatched. When the chemical was banned, the population of eagles began to increase.

Air Pollution

There are many kinds of air pollution. One of the most common forms is smog, which is a combination of smoke and fog. It occurs when **exhaust** from cars, homes, power plants, and factories mix with **moisture** in the air.

Smog hangs over cities like a dark cloud, making it very difficult to see things in the distance. It's usually at its worst on hot summer days, when heat traps pollution from cars and chimneys near the ground.

Smog irritates the eyes, noses, and throats of people and animals. When people breathe in smog over many years, it can harm their lungs and may even cause lung cancer.

People who live in Los Angeles, California, depend heavily on their cars to get around the city. All these cars fill the air with harmful chemicals that are easily trapped in low-lying areas. These factors make Los Angeles one of the smoggiest cities in the United States, even though California has some of the toughest antipollution laws in the country.

A smoggy day in Los Angeles

Freshwater Pollution

For thousands of years, people have used water from rivers and wells for drinking, washing, and cooking. Unfortunately, some of these freshwater sources have become polluted. How?

Farming is the cause of much of the pollution. In order to grow more crops, farmers sometimes use fertilizers and pesticides on their fields. When it rains, these chemicals may be washed into nearby rivers. They may also seep deep into the earth, reaching underground sources of water. Freshwater that's polluted by pesticides, fertilizers, and **sewage** can kill wildlife and make the people who use it sick.

Polluted water spewing into a river

The Ganges River

The Ganges River, located in India, is one of the most polluted rivers in the world. The pollution includes sewage, trash, food, and human and animal remains.

Ocean Pollution

People once thought that because the sea is so big, anything dumped into it would just disappear. Unfortunately, this is not true.

Many of the same chemicals that pollute freshwater also end up in the ocean. Fertilizers washed into rivers, for example, may eventually flow into the seas, causing **algae** to grow too quickly. Too much algae can kill some of the plants that many sea creatures depend on for survival.

Between 1956 and 1968, a factory in Japan released mercury, a poisonous metal, directly into the sea. Fish that lived in the water soon became **contaminated** with the mercury. This poison built up in the bodies of people who ate the fish. More than 2,000 people became seriously ill from mercury poisoning. Many of them died.

This factory is where the mercury was released into the sea in Japan.

Oil Spills

Just like chemicals and fertilizers, oil can also pollute rivers and oceans. One kind of ocean pollution is caused by crude oil, which is black, sticky, and deadly to wildlife. How does this oil get in the water? In the past, after huge ships that carried oil across the seas dropped off their cargo, they would wash out their tanks in the ocean—releasing oil. This practice is now illegal, though it still sometimes takes place.

Today, tankers that are full of oil can have accidents. They sink or run **aground**, destroying beaches and killing wildlife. One of the worst oil spills occurred in 1989. The tanker, the *Exxon Valdez*, hit a **reef** in Prince William Sound in Alaska. The oil that spilled from the ship may have killed as many as 500,000 seabirds and other animals.

A bird covered in oil from the Exxon Valdez *spill*

CANADA

UNITED
STATES

N
W · E
S

Alaska   CANADA

Valdez

Pacific
Ocean

Prince William
Sound

Area affected
by oil spill

The oil from the *Exxon Valdez* polluted about 1,300 miles (2,092 km) of coastline.

Land Pollution

Pollution not only harms the air and water—it also affects life on land. Weed killers, for example, are used to destroy plants that harm crops. However, these poisons also kill some plants that are not harmful. When these plants are killed, there is less food for insects, many of whom starve to death. Soon, small **mammals**, birds, and spiders that feed on the insects don't have enough food. Eventually, all animal life is affected in some way.

Some chemicals sprayed on land can be spread by the wind. Scientists worry that these chemicals may make people sick if they end up on crops or in meat from animals that ate the contaminated crops.

A farmer spraying his crops with pesticides

Landfills

Garbage is also a major cause of land pollution. Each person in the United States produces a lot of it, about 4 pounds (2 kg) a day. Where does it go?

Many cities dump garbage in big holes in the ground called landfills. When these holes are full, they're covered with soil and then grass is planted on top. Is this a good idea? No! Garbage often contains chemicals from household cleaning products and other sources that contaminate the ground, as well as underground water. Today, many cities line landfills with clay and plastic sheets to help stop chemicals from leaking into the soil.

Rotting food and other **organic waste** in landfills also cause pollution. As these things rot, they produce methane—a **greenhouse gas**. Many scientists think that too much of this and other gases in the atmosphere are causing Earth's air and water to warm up. This is called **global warming**. Many plants and animals will not survive if their homes become too warm.

Garbage being emptied into a landfill

About 55 percent of the garbage in the United States is put in landfills. The rest is **recycled** or burned, which causes air pollution unless the smoke is cleaned before being released.

Bottles being recycled

Radioactive Pollution

Nuclear power, which is considered a **clean energy** source, is made from **radioactive** materials. It does not involve burning **fossil fuels**, so no greenhouse gases are released into the atmosphere. However, the radioactive materials used to create this power can cause dangerous pollution.

In April 1986, for example, an explosion occurred at the Chernobyl Nuclear Power Plant. Radioactive dust and gas spread through the atmosphere, polluting land and air. Even the rainwater became radioactive. Plants, animals, and people were poisoned. Thirty people died in the explosion. As many as 9,000 people may have passed away from radiation poisoning.

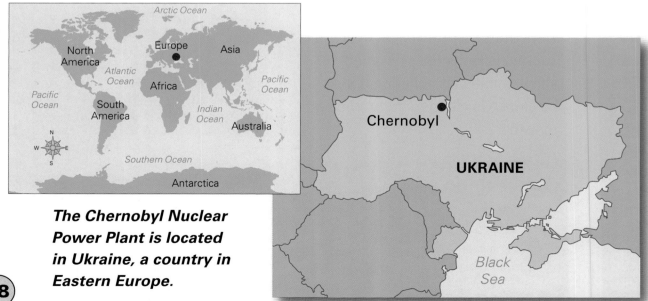

The Chernobyl Nuclear Power Plant is located in Ukraine, a country in Eastern Europe.

The Chernobyl Nuclear Power Plant

All nuclear power stations produce nuclear waste. Some of this waste can stay dangerously radioactive for about 10,000 years. For this reason, it must be carefully buried deep underground in leak-proof containers.

Noise Pollution

The world is a noisy place! Noise can be just as serious as other forms of pollution. Over time, it can damage a person's ability to hear. It can also cause health problems by interfering with a person's concentration and sleep. Most noise pollution is created by machines, especially airplanes, trucks, and cars.

Today more is being done to control noise problems. Barriers, or fences, for example, are built along highways to keep noise away from nearby homes and businesses. Factory equipment and jet engines are designed to operate more quietly than before. Laws are even used to prevent people from bothering their neighbors with loud music and other unwanted sounds.

Bright lights in cities and towns may not seem like a form of pollution, but they are! This type of pollution can disturb sleep and prevent relaxation.

Low-flying planes create a lot of noise.

The Future

In the United States, the government has passed laws to help decrease pollution. For example, in 1963, Congress passed the Clean Air Act to control smog and other kinds of air pollution. This law regulates the waste that can be produced by factories, cars, and other air pollutants.

Cities and towns are also asking people to reduce the amount of garbage they produce by reusing items, such as plastic bottles and paper, that might otherwise be thrown away. They're also requiring that more items be recycled, such as glass, paper, metal, and plastic. If individuals and industries work together, the planet's pollution problems can be solved!

The planet's population is increasing very quickly. More people means there will be more pollution, unless everyone helps keep the environment clean.

Keeping parks clean will help decrease pollution.

Cleaner Energy

There are some ways to produce energy without causing pollution. Here are a few:

- **Wind turbines** are a very clean way of producing energy. One drawback is that they work only in places where the wind blows a lot!

- Solar energy uses light from the sun to make clean energy. Unfortunately, this kind of energy can't be made at night.

- Nuclear power stations don't produce greenhouses gases. They do, however, produce radioactive wastes, which can be very dangerous if they escape into the environment.

- Tidal power uses the movement of the ocean's tides to make clean and reliable energy. However, cities that need this power may be far from the ocean.

Wind turbines

A hydroelectric dam

- **Hydroelectric** power stations use the force of water rushing downhill or the release of water trapped behind dams to make power. However, these kinds of power stations can only be built in areas with mountains or steep hills. Also, some dams are very large and the space they take up can destroy habitats.

Get Out of the Car!

Fumes from cars cause serious pollution. Some people think electric cars may be the best way to reduce pollution produced by gasoline. However, the electricity to charge the cars' batteries usually comes from power stations that burn fossil fuels—which creates air pollution. Even so, electric cars produce less pollution than regular automobiles. So they're a great way to cut down on air pollution.

Here are some ways to reduce pollution from cars and trucks:

- Buy food that is locally grown. It doesn't have to travel long distances, like food grown far away, to get to markets.

- Use public transportation, such as buses and trains.

- Walk or ride a bicycle to get around. It's good for the environment, and it's good for a person's health.

Here are some ways people who drive cars can cut down on pollution:

- Slow down! Driving fast uses more gas than going slowly.

- Drive smaller, more energy-efficient cars—such as hybrids.

- Join a carpool.

Here are some ways carmakers can make cars run cleaner:

- Produce more hybrid cars. These cars use a lot less fuel than regular cars.

- Design cars so engines don't run when a car is standing still.

- Find new, clean fuels that pollute the environment less than present energy sources.

Organic Farming

Most shops and supermarkets sell **organic foods** such as fruits, vegetables, and meat. How are these foods better than nonorganic items?

- Organic fruits, vegetables, and meat are produced in a natural way. The soil that the fruits and vegetables are grown in is not treated with chemical pesticides and fertilizers. The animals are not given chemicals to make them grow bigger.

- Organic fruits and vegetables cost more than nonorganic foods in markets. So why don't people grow their own? Even a small garden can produce a few vegetables. If a person doesn't have space for a garden, small salad vegetables, such as tomatoes and cucumbers, can be grown in a window box, or even in a flowerpot on a windowsill. Growing things to eat is fun—and they taste great!

Clean Rivers: The Cuyahoga River Fire, A Case Study

The Cuyahoga River in Ohio has been an important shipping route for many years. It was, at one time, incredibly polluted, too. In fact, it was once so contaminated that it actually caught fire!

In 1969, an oil slick on the river burst into flames near Cleveland, Ohio. The fire may have been started by a spark from a passing train. Fueled by oil and other pollutants, the fire burned for about 25 minutes.

The Cuyahoga is not the only polluted river that has caught on fire, but it's one that received a lot of attention. The day after the fire, the local fire chief told newspapers that businesses on the water had caused the fire because they often dumped oil into the water and didn't clean it up.

The fire made people aware of industrial pollution. To prevent such a disaster from happening again, the U.S. government set up the Environmental Protection Agency (EPA) in 1970. Congress also passed the Clean Water Act of 1972. Today, the Cuyahoga is no longer as polluted as it was in 1969. It's getting cleaner all the time.

The Cuyahoga River today

Deadly Litter

Litter makes parks, beaches, forests, and other areas look terrible. It can also be deadly to wildlife. Here are a few ways that garbage can harm living things.

- Small animals sometimes climb into glass or plastic bottles. If the insides of the bottles are too slippery for them to escape, they can starve to death inside.

- Land animals can get their heads stuck in plastic cartons or in the plastic rings that are used to carry bottles or cans. These items can choke even a small animal.

- When animals swallow broken glass, it can cut their insides as it passes through their bodies.

- A piece of glass lying in a field or a forest can act like a magnifying glass when sunlight passes through it, which can start a fire.

- Remember, glass and plastic don't rot. When placed in landfills, they may last thousands of years! That's why all glass and plastic should be reused or recycled.

Birds and sea creatures swallow bits of plastic floating in water. They may choke on these pieces. The animals can also get stuck inside larger plastic items and either suffocate or drown.

Making Laws

One of the best ways to stop pollution is to get the government to keep making laws. Laws against polluting the air, land, and water are very strict. If you break them, you might have to pay a large fine. If the pollution happens on a big enough scale, it might even mean serving time in jail.

Antarctica is the cleanest place on Earth. Fortunately, it's protected by strong antipollution laws. Without these laws, however, the land and the seas around it could become seriously polluted.

Even in Antarctica, however, there is an area that is not very clean. Wilkes Station opened in 1957. Over the years, it has become a mess. The station was contaminated by leaking fuel containers and closed down in 1969. It has been buried under ice for years. However, sometimes during a thaw, you can see some of the old buildings and the garbage that was left behind! People are now working hard to clean up this area.

There has been a lot of garbage found at Wilkes Station.

How to Help

Everyone needs to get involved to help reduce pollution. Here are some things to do.

- With the help of a teacher or another responsible adult, collect litter around your school. Do not handle broken glass, sharp cans, or other dangerous objects. Figure out how much of the litter collected can be recycled. Then recycle it.

- Find out how pollution problems are tackled in your neighborhood and what you can do to help fix the problems.

- Ask your parents and other adults to buy food that is produced locally and doesn't have too much packaging. Also, try to eat organic food as often as possible.

- Always recycle! Make sure that any waste, such as paper and plastics, are put in proper containers.

Learn More Online

To learn more about pollution, visit
www.bearportpublishing.com/EarthinDanger

Glossary

aground (uh-GROUND) to get stuck on the bottom of the ocean near the shore in shallow water; parts of the ships that run aground are often punctured, causing leaks

algae (AL-jee) a kind of tiny plant that lives mainly in the water and makes food using energy from the sun

atmosphere (AT-muhss-fihr) the mixture of gases surrounding Earth

clean energy (KLEEN EN-ur-jee) a type of power that produces little or no polluting gases, such as carbon dioxide, during use

contaminated (kuhn-TAM-uh-nate-id) made dirty or unfit for use

exhaust (eg-ZAWST) smoke and other gases released when fossil fuels burn

fertilizers (FUR-tuh-*lize*-urz) materials that are rich in substances that help plants grow

fossil fuels (FOSS-uhl FYOO-uhlz) fuels such as coal, oil, and gas made from the remains of plants and animals that died millions of years ago

global warming (GLOHB-uhl WORM-ing) the gradual heating up of Earth's air and water caused by a buildup of greenhouse gases that trap heat from the sun in Earth's atmosphere

greenhouse gas (GREEN-*houss* GASS) a gas, such as carbon dioxide or methane, that traps warm air in the atmosphere

hydroelectric (*hye*-droh-i-LEK-trik) the production of electricity by using moving water to turn a generator

mammals (MAM-uhlz) animals that are warm-blooded, nurse their young with milk, and have hair or fur on their skin

moisture (MOIS-chur) any form of water, including water vapor

organic foods (or-GAN-ik FOODZ) food grown without using chemical fertilizers or pesticides

organic waste (or-GAN-ik WAYST) garbage that comes from things that were once alive

pesticides (PESS-tuh-*sidez*) chemicals used to kill insects and other pests that damage crops

pollute (puh-LOOT) to allow harmful materials, such as oils, wastes, and chemicals, to damage the air, water, or land

radioactive (*ray*-dee-oh-AK-tiv) giving off dangerous, invisible rays of energy

recycled (ree-SYE-kuhld) when used, old, and unwanted objects are turned into something new and useful

reef (REEF) a ridge of rock, sand, or coral that lies near the surface of a body of water

sewage (SOO-ij) liquid and solid wastes that go down drains

wind turbines (WIND TUR-binez) machines resembling windmills that turn the power of the wind into electricity

Index

Read More

Donald, Rhonda Lucas. *Water Pollution.* Danbury, CT: Children's Press (2001).

National Wildlife Federation. *Pollution: Problems & Solutions.* New York: McGraw-Hill (1998).